TEDDINGTON AS IT WAS

Researched and compiled by members of
The Teddington Society

Front Cover: Park Road in 1900. Mr Last's Cash Drug Store advertises the *Daily Telegraph*. On the other side of The causeway is the wall of Teddington Lodge, now the site of the Police Station. In front of the wall is the drinking fountain erected to celebrate Queen Victoria's Golden Jubilee in 1887. The Clarence Hotel is on the left. Some of the decoration has now gone and it was renamed The Park in 2001.

First edition, November 1980
Second impression, October 1983
Third impression, September 1987
Fourth impression, September 1991
Fifth impression, April 2002

Published by Hendon Publishing Company Limited, Hendon Mill, Nelson, Lancashire.
Text © The Teddington Society, 1980.
Printed by Fretwell Print and Design Limited, Goulbourne Street, Keighley, West Yorkshire BD21 1PZ.

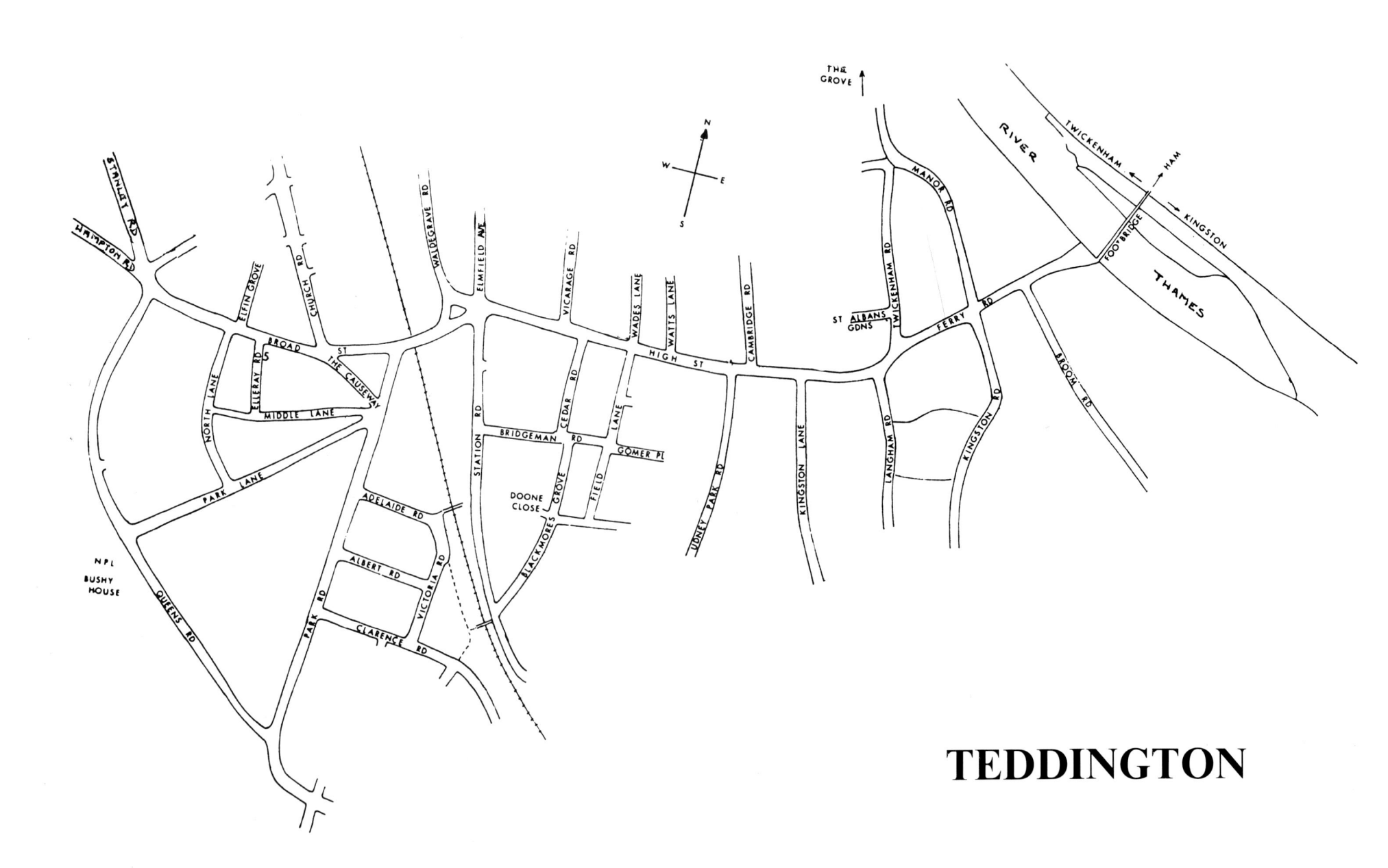

TEDDINGTON

Teddington High Street runs straight through our town eastwards towards the Thames. Here it is marked conspicuously by the new tramlines in 1903. 'The Royal Oak' on the left, has been a public house since the beginning of the 18th century and possibly earlier. It was rebuilt back from the road in the 1930s.

Bridgman House. Orlando Bridgman (1606–74) spent his last years in Teddington with his family and chaplain, Thomas Traherne, the metaphysical poet. As an eminent and impartial lawyer he was appointed by Charles II to re-apportion Royalist estates after the Commonwealth. He is buried in St. Mary's Church. His house, much altered, with a third storey, became latterly a club for St Albans Church before it was demolished in 1911. The Telephone Exchange now occupies the site.

Lemons Bakery 1908. Old houses in the High Street had shops built on their front gardens. Lemons catered for the wealthy at the turn of the century as 'complete furnisher for Banquets, Balls, Weddings etc' which functions were popular and frequent. The building on the right is still standing.

This interesting collection of roof-tops belonged to Lemons Bakery and was photographed in 1908 to illustrate the adaptation of much earlier premises.

Queen Elizabeth's Hunting Lodge. This house dates from 1564 and was reputedly used by guests from Hampton Court. A letter from the Earl of Leicester to the Queen dated 1570 is from Teddington. Much altered, as here, it survived till 1875 when it was demolished for the construction of Udney Park Road. The village maypole stood opposite the house.

Udney House. This photograph is said to be of Udney House, Teddington but it is not the house of the same name which was on the corner of Kingston Lane until it was demolished in 1898. Robert Udney lived in Teddington from 1790 until his death in 1802. He was a successful West India merchant and a connoisseur of art. His extensive collection of mainly Italian paintings was sold after his death and many of the pictures he owned hang in important galleries today. The picture gallery, which was demolished before the house, may have been a detached building on the High Street.

Teddington Place was built in about 1700 by Sir Charles Duncombe, who became Lord Mayor of London. The house was decorated by Verrio and Grinling Gibbons who both worked nearby at Hampton Court. The house stood in the present Udney Park Gardens and its grounds reached as far as Kingston Road. The house was enlarged over the years but was not finally demolished until 1946. Langham Road passes through the former grounds and St Albans Church was built on part of the gardens. At the end of the 19th century, it was confusingly known as Udney Hall.

The Drawing Room of Teddington Place here displays its Edwardian splendour with chaise-longue, chandeliers, dried grass and bullrushes.

Building the Lock. In the eighteenth century, because the Thames became short of water for increasing navigation, a locking plan was adopted. By 1811 the first lock at Teddington was completed to improve conditions upstream.

Teddington Weir was completed in 1812. By 1853 the river was suffering from increased extraction upstream and the lock had to be rebuilt. By 1904 there were three locks, the largest able to accommodate a tug and six barges.

Fishing at the Weir. The Weir was a much favoured fishing ground. Top hats, frock coats and clay pipes seem to be *de rigeur*. The dredger in the background was constantly at work, clearing the channel.

Busy Day. Holiday time at the turn of the century would see the locks and 'rollers' full of craft of varying sizes and boatmen of varying skill, while crowds gathered to watch. A craze for boating had developed and a special style of river gear was practically compulsory.

Before the Suspension Bridge. A bridge linking the Surrey and Middlesex riversides was built in 1877. Here is the beach on the Middlesex bank before the building of the bridge, with Mr Norris Senior and his son, both of whom worked in the candle factory.

The Anglers Hotel on the Middlesex Bank close to the Suspension Bridge. This was a favourite resort for river users in search of refreshment.

The Little Ships setting out for Dunkirk in May 1940, from Tough's boat yard. Many returned here for repair after the expedition.

An aerial view of Broom Road and Teddington Lock and Weir in 1924. The two large houses on the river bank to the right of the picture are 'Old Broom Hall' and 'Broom Hall'. Those in Broom Road approaching the Lock are 'Weir House' and 'Dunbar House', now the Lensbury Club. Thames Television Studios now occupy the next two sites of 'Rock Hall' and 'Weir House'. Across the river the land is still being farmed.

St Mary's Churchyard and Church House. The view on the left looks across the churchyard to the church and to Church House. The house was demolished about 1900 when the road was widened to accommodate the electric trams.

The photo on the right shows the church tower with its cupola which is no longer there. There was a church here in the 13th century which replaced an earlier chapel but the earliest part of the church standing today dates from the 16th century. The church tower was paid for by Dr Stephen Hales, the scientist and inventor who was the minister here from 1709 until his death in 1761.

This Manor House is said to have been rebuilt in about 1800 but an older house, possibly built in the 16th century, can be seen behind the brickwork. The Manor of Teddington had been the property of Westminster Abbey but was appropriated by Henry VIII as part of the Honour of Hampton Court until it became an independent manor in 1603. The manor was broken up in 1862 when most of the land in Teddington was sold for development. The lord of the manor lived at the Manor House until 1729 after which the property was let to tenants.

The Grove. This house stood in the Twickenham Road on the site of the present Grove Estate and its grounds stretched down to the river. The house was built for Moses Franks, one of the respected and wealthy Jews living in the area. Sir William Chambers, the architect, was involved with the design, probably of the garden. One of the more famous owners was John Walter, the founder of the *Universal Daily Register*, later to become *The Times*, who lived here from 1797 to 1812. This picture in 1907 shows a hospital fund raising fete.

The Grove Boat House, 1890. Most riverside houses had substantial boat houses. The Grove had a tunnel under Twickenham Road to connect the lawn by the river with the house. Mr Strachan, who owned the house in the mid-nineteenth century, received his guests this way when they arrived by water from Kingston and Richmond. Many of them were coming to conferences of the Church Missionary Society.

Peg Woffington has no documental contact with these cottages which are erroneously regarded as her gift to the poor. Peg had a short but brilliant career on the London stage and spent some of her last years in Teddington, dying when only 39. She is buried in St Mary's Church and has a memorial plaque there. The cottages bear a date of 1759 but there is proof of earlier structures, possibly Elizabethan.

Faversham House opposite the cottages, of late 17th century origin formed part of Sir Charles Duncombe's estate. In the latter half of the 19th century it was used as a school for young ladies run by Miss Elizabeth Acton. It was acquired by St Alban's Church in the 1890s and was run as an evening institute. It was demolished in 1918.

The King's Head, an old hostelry, dates from the 17th century. The 'head' referred to is that of Charles I. Today it is still standing but has a different frontage. In 1865 the last Court Leet of the Manor of Teddington was held here after which local government of the village was transferred to the Local Board.

St Mary's Vicarage. The vicarage was built by public subscription in 1838 because it was thought essential that the village should provide the minister with a house. It was some way from the church and was sold in 1881. The house on the left was demolished to make way for Vicarage Road. The vicarage was used as the post office, a grocers and drapers and the shops were later built out on the front gardens as they are today, but the old house is still standing.

Louisa and Sally Barber.

Teddington Dairy on the opposite corner of Vicarage Road has a unique history. Villagers were served with dairy produce from 1819 onwards by 'cow-keepers', who herded cattle in fields near the High Street. In 1874 two enterprising country girls Louisa and Sally Barber came to Teddington and married Mr Roberts and Mr Prewett, and set out to improve the dairy business. By 1899 Louisa had married her second husband Mr Job and assured the success of Job's Dairy for many years.

Teddington House. This pleasant and extensive house was built about 1750 at the west end of the High Street. The site is now occupied by the Post Office Sorting Office and Elmfield Avenue.

Percy Lodge with its attractive façade stood next door to Teddington House. It was the home of Stephen Hales, one of Teddington's most famous residents. Dr Hales was Vicar of St Mary's Church, a scientist and innovator, with an interest in hygiene and people. He is distinguished as a founder member of the Royal Society of Arts and as a member of the Royal Society.

Elmfield House was probably built about 1690 at the west end of the village. The sale catalogue of 1824 includes a drawing of the house with the Mound, willow trees and a pond. The artist may have exaggerated its merits as he seems to have exaggerated its perspective. In about 1815 was acquired by Alexander Barclay who opened the wax factory behind the house. One tenant of note, Alexander Herzen, entertained Garibaldi here on 17 April 1864.

The house stills stands today but it lost its iron gateway in 1927 for road widening and the chimneys in 1956 for safety reasons. The house was purchased in 1895, after much opposition, by the Local Board for Council offices and it has remained in the hands of the Council ever since. First the UDC until 1937 when Teddington was amalgamated with the Borough of Twickenham and by the Greater London Borough of Richmond On Thames since 1965. Some features, both inside and out have changed little since the house was built.

Waldegrave Road to the west of Elmfield House is today much wider, here the road is only a dirt track. In the middle distance we see the wax candle factory chimney. In the 18th and 19th centuries the finest, white wax was made here and bleached in adjacent fields; it even fulfilled the high standard of Vatican demands. The factory was guarded by geese. The Paint Research Association now occupies this site which is next to the Public Library. The building in the right foreground is thought to be the old coach house and stables of Elmfield House and blocks a sight of the old Fire Station.

The Elm Tree. This magnificent tree stood in Station Road meadows, opposite Elmfield House, to which it may have given its name. It was felled in 1930. The building operation in the right background forecasts the erection of the Savoy Cinema.

Gomer House. R.D. Blackmore (1825–1900), author of 'Lorna Doone' and about fourteen less famous novels, lived at Gomer House, off Station Road, from 1868 to 1900. Poor health and a timely legacy induced him to take up market gardening, but this did not prove to be very profitable and was subsidised with his income from writing. His observations on rainfall and fruit marketing make interesting reading.

The Blackmore Procession, 1925. This procession celebrated the centenary of Blackmore's birth and attended a memorial service for him at St Mary's Church. Twickenham councillors head the procession, Dr John Leeson, in top hat, the Charter Mayor is accompanied by Mrs Leeson and behind him is Mr Richard Blewett, senior reporter on the Richmond and Twickenham Times.

Bridge Approach. The centre of Teddington by 1903 looks very different from the rural delights shown previously. Elmfield House is still to the right of the picture. The 'Mount' was replaced by the Railway Bridge, when the pond was drained in 1863. The Bridge stretched westward from Waldegrave Road to Church Road. By 1903 the London Electric Tramway ran along the main street.

Broad Street. This view looking east towards The Causeway was taken after the Tramway was established in 1903. The 'Northampton Arms' on the left was an ale house which closed about 1910. Phelps on the right was a large furniture store, now the site of Tesco.

Broad Street showing some of the American Buildings. These were some of the earliest houses in the road, built in 1828 and were called 'Botany Bay' and 'The New Maid Homes'. The following year they were called 'Mr Young's American Buildings' but the reason for this is not known. In 1828 there were a few larger houses at the west end of Broad Street which are still there hidden behind the shops which by the end of the century had invaded the street.

The Public School about 1865. A school for about sixty boys was built in 1832, for which about £500 was raised. Beside the school was a house for the master and a shed for the fire engine. Queen Adelaide contributed £100 and the fact was commemorated on the school wall.

The Girls School. By 1843 space was found for girls and infants. Their building adjoined the boy's school. It was enlarged in 1868 and the whole complex demolished in 1979.

Collis School. A typical classroom photograph taken about 1908 at the school started by Miss Sarah Collis, under the auspices of Christchurch. A charge of two pence per week was made. It catered for girls and had also an Infants department.

St Alban's Church on the opposite side of the road to St Mary's, was built in 1887 by public subscription to replace St Mary's, which was too small for Teddington congregations. Subscriptions were enthusiastically given and gathered – in fact more was subscribed than expected. Stone was substituted for brick and the great French Gothic Church became a conspicuous sight from far away with its gleaming green copper roof. It proved a very popular venture – people came from long distances and carriages lined the streets during services.

But enthusiasm waned as the years passed – congregations fell away. Some parts of the Church were never completed. The church was declared redundant in the 1970s and the congregation was rehoused in the old church now called St Mary's with St Alban's. The Landmark Trust now uses the gutted St Alban's building as a centre for the performing arts.

St Peter & St Paul's Church was built in 1865 at the corner of Church Road. It was to cater for the increasing population at this end of the town. This area in 1865 still had a very rural air, with no sign of the shopping complex which was to follow. The Church was demolished in 1979.

The Public Library. In the Broad Street, a section of Elfin Villas on the north side was taken over to accommodate a modest Public Library in 1900. The Public Library served till 1906 when it was replaced by the Carnegie Library in Waldegrave Road.

The Fishmonger at the western end of Broad Street about 1900, displays his Christmas stock.

Honey's Shop stood at the corner of Broad street and Queens Road. Mr Honey and his two daughters sold 'everything', kettles, shag, pegs, peas and paraffin. Pinks' Jam is being delivered; Shepherds Bush Empire is advertised opposite. The Wesleyan Chapel, destroyed in the Second World War, is in the centre, with Hampton Road on the left going to Hampton and Stanley Road on the right going to Twickenham.

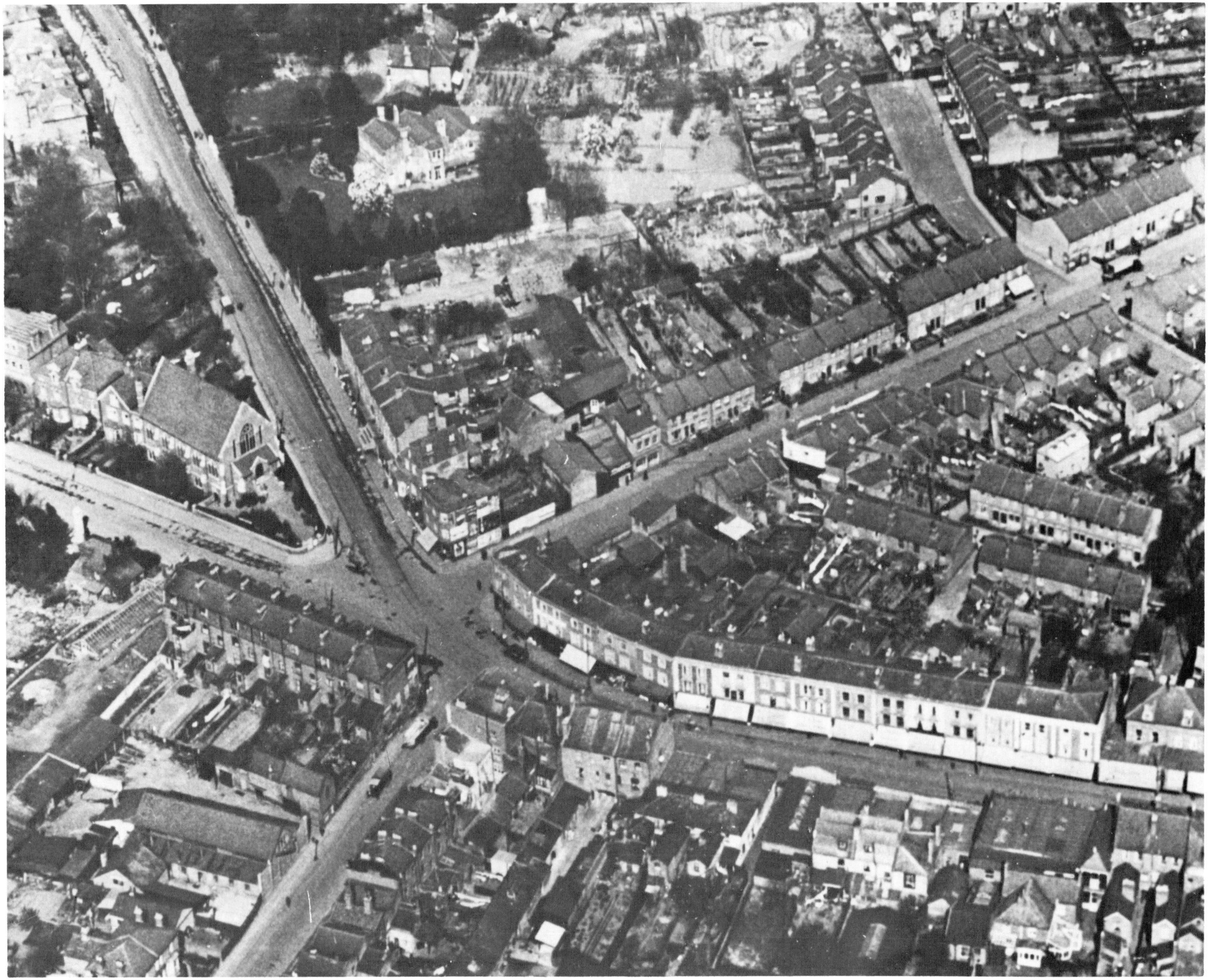

The Old Cottage Hospital was in Elfin Grove off Broad Street. It was supported by voluntary contributions. Hospital Sunday, 1907, was the occasion for a fund collecting procession, here passing the Royal Oak on its way round the town. A new hospital was essential and was financed by voluntary contributions; it rose on the Anderson Nursery site in 1929 as a War Memorial.

Opposite: This aerial photograph taken in 1928 shows the five road junction at the Wesleyan Chapel. Considerable bomb damage was done here in the Second World War and the chapel and most of the property on the east side of Stanley Road was badly damaged and subsequently demolished. Today there is no vehicular access between Walpole Road and Stanley Road and the houses have been replaced with flats. A configuration of traffic lights now adorns the junction.

Sister Stone was the district nurse for Teddington in the early twentieth century. She travelled to her patients from one end of the town to another by tram or on foot. She sits here in her sitting room, very upright with her souvenirs and presents around her. She knew many young people in the town, having brought them into the world. She died, in retirement, in 1942.

Hampton Road. This cottage next to the barn was occupied until 1935 when it was demolished. It was for many years in the nineteenth century the only habitation between Anderson's Nursery and Hampton Hill. The Furze field was used for cultivation and seasonal pea-pickers would camp here in their dark tents, frightening the villagers. The National Physical Laboratory acquired the land in 1921.

Hampton Road. Large houses were built in Hampton Road about 1900, with extensive walled gardens. Roads remained dirt tracks but here pavements were laid for 'starched' nurses and babies on their way to the Park.

The Causeway, formerly called Wolsey Road, joined Park Road and Broad Street and was opened in about 1860. The later name would appear to indicate the regular occurrence of flooding.

The Town Hall. The exuberance of life in Teddington in the late Victorian period was typified in 1886 when Mr Collier, a builder, began building his Town Hall in the Causeway. It provided parochial offices, a ballroom, a billiard room, a theatre and some shops. During the building Mr Collier and some workmen were injured by the collapse of a window arch insufficiently dried out. In July 1887 his daughter laid the foundation stone. When this picture was taken *Trilby* was being performed.

On 29th December 1903 the Town Hall, which had been a limited success, was burnt down and never rebuilt.

The Almshouses. A row of almshouses, 42–50 Park Lane, was built in 1739, with money provided by a bequest from Sir Francis Bridgeman, the son of Sir Orlando and Lady Dorothy Bridgeman, and other private contributions. They were built for the accommodation of poor families. A workhouse was later built beside them but this did not survive for long and the poor of the parish were sent to Hampton Workhouse. The almshouses were demolished in 1950.

Park Lane. This house, Adelaide House, one of a pair of early or pre-19th century houses, stands at the corner of Park Lane and Park Road. The lane led to a complex of cottage dwellings associated with a farming area and to the almshouses. It also led to Bushy House which in 1900 became the National Physical Laboratory.

James's Farm. A photograph taken about 1870 shows one of the last farms in Teddington; James had a very large farm stretching on both sides of Hampton Road with pasture and arable. The yard probably occupied the site of the Car Park and Council Store in North Lane. James became associated with Edwards, another dairy farmer, who used fields in Coleshill Road and had a dairy and shop in Broad Street until 1931.

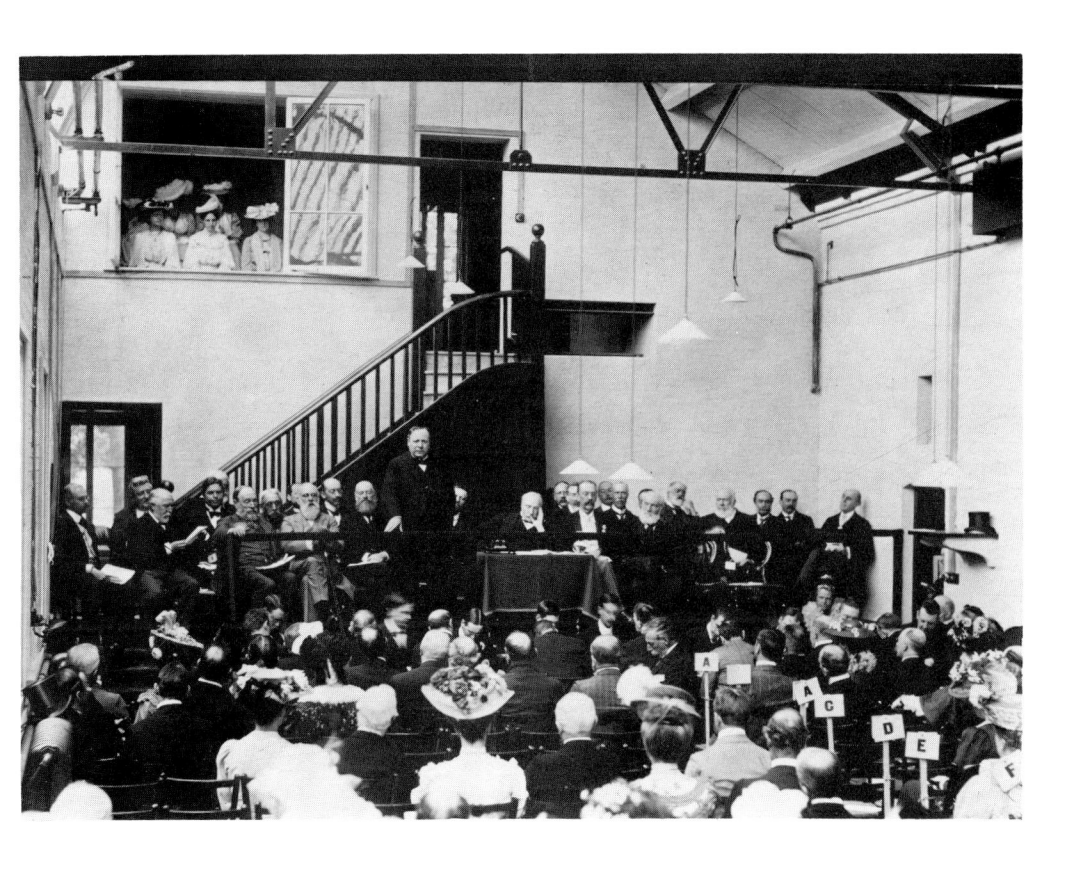

Kitchen of Bushy House. This famous house, home of Lord North, The Duke of Clarence, Mrs Jordan, Queen Adelaide and many others had been allotted, with Victoria's approval to the Royal Society for a National Physical Laboratory. In the picture the Electronics Department is entertaining guests for an opening ceremony in 1906, in very crowded quarters.

The Metallurgical Department. This picture in 1908 shows the old kitchen of Bushy House forced into unusual service till a more suitable building could be found in 1911. Soon 'the Lab' expanded into the grounds of the House and later into fields to the east, where space was available for purpose-built accommodation.

Queen's Road, on a hot summer's day, was a pleasant shady walk past the Laboratory entrance, here in the middle distance. The milkman serves his customers from a large can covered with a canvas jacket to keep it cool. A gravel path to the left beyond him followed a stream, with tadpoles and minnows and wild flowers, which led to an iron gate into Bushy Park. This gate still exists though it is now reached from Coleshill Road.

Cannon Gate. The gate to Bushy House from Bushy Park was guarded by cannon, probably from the Crimean campaign. They were sacrificed for munitions in the Second World War.

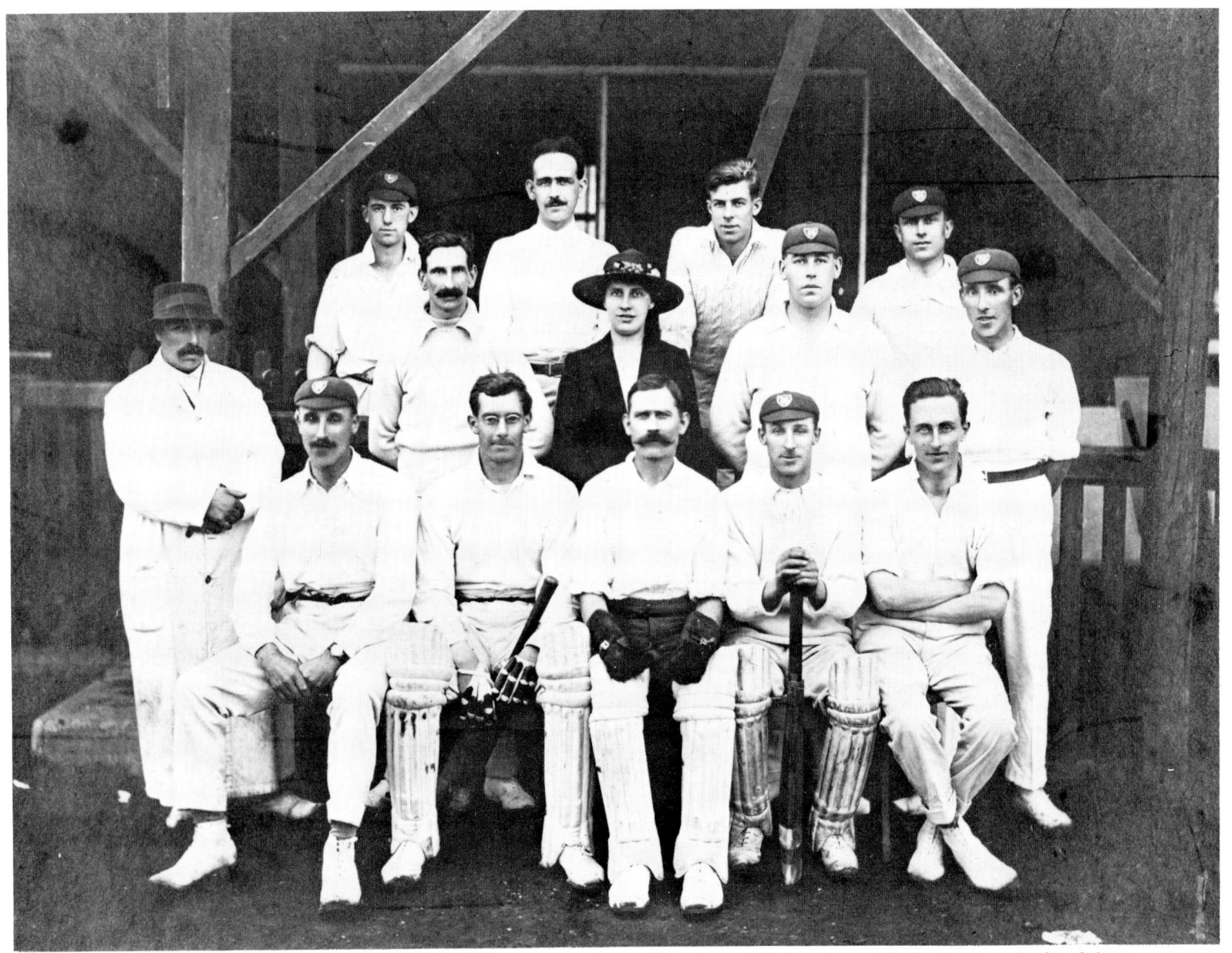

Teddington Town Cricket Club. Originating in 1891 from members of the choir of St Peter's and St Paul's Church, the club was largely made up of the tradesmen of the town and played its fixtures on Sunday and Wednesday afternoons. At one time it was known as Upper Teddington Cricket Club and changed to the present title after the First World War. There is some mention of the club moving to its present site in Bushy Park when the railway came to town but as the latter occurred in 1864 and the club was not founded until 1891, this has become confused with the history of their older neighbours, Teddington Cricket Club.

This photograph taken about 1924 shows:

Back Row	unknown	Fred Hawkins	unknown	Allan Cleveland	
Middle Row	unknown	? Llewellyn	Mrs Smith	a policeman	Smith
Front Row	Alf Smith	Oscar Chilcot	"Wacker" Thomas	Smith	unknown

Cycling in Bushy Park. The height of the cycling craze was from 1874–82 when Bushy Park became the rendez-vous for club meetings. Here we see a procession from Hampton Court encircling the Diana fountain and rejoining amidst cheering crowds. In 1880, 2,000 cyclists were joined by 2,000 spectators. In 1882, 183 clubs took part. Such enormous numbers proved too much for the organisers and the meetings were abandoned in favour of smaller groups. From 1884–7 the tricyclists took over, but the glamour had gone.

Bushy Park Cottage 1900; an interesting creeper covered house built about the same time as Bushy Lodge. It still stands, but here we see it about 1900 with its elderly resident, her companion and a parrot.

Bushy Lodge. This impressive house faced Chestnut Avenue in Bushy Park. It was possibly built in about 1815 and was altered at a later date. Built in nine acres of land, it had several large reception rooms, a billiard room, an Adam style drawing room and twelve bedrooms besides servants quarters. The house was occupied by Miss Elizabeth and Miss Isabella Mercer until about 1865. For a few years before it was demolished in 1925, it was occupied as the Twilight Sleep Nursing Home and might have become the new Cottage Hospital but the accommodation was considered unsuitable. Now only the former gatehouse survives.

The Adelaide Inn is named after William IV's Widow, Queen Adelaide, who as Ranger of Bushy Park, lived for many years at Bushy House. She was a much loved patroness of the Church and Teddington School.

The inn, 'a good call for cricketers and cyclists' was built about 1860 and survives today very much unaltered although it no longer sells theatre programmes, railway tickets and trips.

The Oriental Car ready to join a procession in 1902, for a celebration of Edward VII's coronation. The participants have gathered at the Adelaide.

Park Road 1863. This view taken soon after the opening of the railway shows the houses left of the lower level when the bridge was built. Mr Reed, the grocer, occupied the first house on the left and as well as his groceries also sold cloth. The tall building in the distance is the Clarence Arms.

Coronation Procession, 1910. This procession of happy children is just passing the Clarence Hotel and is celebrating the coronation of King George V.